Book 1
C++ Programming Professional
Made Easy
BY SAM KEY

&

Book 2

Facebook Social Power
BY SAM KEY

Book 1
C++ Programming Professional Made Easy
BY SAM KEY

Expert C++ Programming Language Success in a Day for Any Computer User!

Programming Box Set #56: C++ Programming Professional Made Easy & Facebook Social Power

Table Of Contents

Introduction

I want to thank you and congratulate you for purchasing the book, "Professional C++ Programming Made Easy".

This book contains proven steps and strategies on how to learn the C++ programming language as well as its applications.

There's no need to be a professional developer to code quick and simple C++ programs. With this book, anyone with basic computer knowledge can explore and enjoy the power of the *C++ Programming Language*. Included are the following fundamental topics for any beginner to start coding *today:*

- The basic C++ terms

- Understanding the C++ Program Structure

- Working with Variables, Expressions, and Operators

- Using the Input and Output Stream for User Interaction

- Creating Logical Comparisons

- Creating Loops and Using Condition Statements

- And Many More!

Thanks again for purchasing this book, I hope you enjoy it!

Chapter 1 – Introduction to C++

What You Will Learn:

***A Brief History of the C++ Language**

***C++ Basic Terminology**

***C++ Program Structure**

C++ is one of the most popular programming languages that people are using today. More specifically, C++ is a library of "commands" that tell your computer what to do and how to do it. These commands make up the C++ *source code*.

Take note that C++ is different from the C programming language that came before it. In fact, it is supposedly better version of the C language when *Bjarne Stroustrup* created it back in 1983.

Even today, the C++ language serves as the "starting point" for many experts in the world of programming. Although it is particularly easy to learn and apply, the ceiling for C++ mastery is incredibly high.

C++ Basic Terminology

Of course, the first step in learning the C++ programming language is to understand the basic terms. To prevent any unnecessary confusion at any point as you read this book, this section explains the most commonly used terms in the C++ program syntax. Just like the entire programming language itself, most terms in C++ are easy to remember and understand.

Compiler

Before anything else, take note that a compiler is needed to run the codes you've written with C++. Think of compilers as "translators" that convert programming language into *machine language* – the language that a computer understands. The machine language consists of only two characters (1s and 0s), which is why it is also called as *binary language.* If you're learning C++ at school, then you shouldn't worry about getting a compiler for C++ *or* an *Integrated Development Environment* for that matter.

Integrated Development Environment

An Integrated Development Environment (IDE) is essentially the software you're using to write C++ programs. It only makes sense for IDEs to come with compilers needed to run your codes. If you have no experience with C++ programming and attempting to learn it on your own, you can opt for a free C++ IDE such as *Code::Blocks.* A good choice for complete beginners is to opt for a simple C++ IDE such as *Quincy 2005* since there is very little setup required.

Variables and Parameters

Variables are individual blocks in the program's memory that contains a given value. A value may be set as a constant, determined by the value of other variables using operators, or set/changed through user input. Variables are denoted by variable names or *identifiers.* In programming with C++, you can use any variable name you desire as long as all characters are valid. Remember that only alphanumeric characters and "underscores" (_) can be used in identifiers. Punctuation marks and other symbols are not allowed.

Keep in mind that variables always need to be *declared* first before they can be used. Declaring variables are different from deciding their actual values; meaning both processes are done in two different codes. These processes will be explained in the next chapter.

"Parameters" work the same way as regular variables. In fact, they are even written in the same syntax. However, parameters and variables are initialized in different ways. Parameters are specifically included in *functions* to allow arguments to be passed to a separate location from which the functions are called.

Statements

Every program written with C++ consists of different lines of code that performs tasks such as setting variables, calling functions, and other expressions. These lines are *statements*. Each individual statement always ends with a semicolon (;). More importantly, statements in a function are executed chronologically based on which comes first. Of course, this order can be altered using *flow control statements* such as "if statements" and "loops".

Functions

Functions are blocks in a C++ program structured to complete a single task. You can call upon functions at any point whilst the program is running. Curly brackets or braces ({}) enclose the statements or "body" in each function. Aside from a function name, functions are also set with corresponding "types" which refer to the requested form of *returned value*. You can also use and set parameters at the beginning of each function. They are enclosed in parentheses "()" and separated using commas (,).

In C++, the following is the most used syntax when creating functions:

"type" "name" (parameter 1, parameter 2, parameter 3, ...)
{
        "statements";
}

Comments

When working on particularly bigger projects, most experienced programmers use "comments" that can be used as descriptions for specific sections in a C++ program. Comments are completely ignored by a compiler and can therefore ignore proper coding syntax. Comments are preceded either by a *two slashes* (//) or a *slash-asterisk* (/*). You will find comments in the examples throughout this book to help you understand them. A quick example would be the *"Hello World!"* program below. Of course, you can also use comments in your future projects for reference and debugging purposes.

8

Programming Box Set #56: C++ Programming Professional Made Easy & Facebook Social Power

The C++ Program Structure

The program structure of C++ is very easy to understand. The compiler reads every line of code from top to bottom. This is why the first part of a C++ program usually starts with *preprocessor directives* and the declaration of variables and their values. The best way to illustrate this structure is to use the most popular example in the world of C++ -- the "Hello World!" program. Take note of the lines of code as well as the comments below:

#include <iostream> // this is a preprocessor directive

int main() // this line initiates the function named main, which should be found in every C++ program

{

> **std::cout << "Hello World!";** // the statements found between the curly braces make up the main function's body
>
> **return 0;** // the return 0; statement is required to tell the program that the function ran correctly. However, some compilers do not require this line in the main function

}

The topmost line ("#include <iostream>") is a preprocessor directive that defines a section of the standard C++ programming library known as the Input/Output Stream or simply *iostream*. This section handles the input and output operations in C++ programs. Remember that this is important if you wish to use "std::cout" in the main function's body.

The first line "int main ()" initializes the main function. Remember that the "int" refers to the *integer* data type and he "main" refers to the function's name. There are other data types aside from int. But you should focus on the integer data type for now. Since the "Hello World!" program does not need a parameter, it leaves the space between the parentheses succeeding the function name blank. Also, bear in mind that you should NOT place a semicolon (;) after initializing functions.

Next is the function's body, denoted by the open curly brace. This particular part ("std::cout") of the program refers to the **standard** character **out**put device, which is the computer's display device. Next comes the *insertion operator* (<<) from the input/output stream which means the rest of the line is to be outputted (excluding quotations). Lastly, the statement is closed with a semicolon (;).

The last line in the function's body is the *return statement* ("return = 0;"). Remember that the return expression (in this example, "0") depends on the data type specified upon initialization of the function. However, it is possible to create functions without the need for return statements using the "void" function type. For example; *void main ()*.

An alternate way to do this is to include the line "using namespace std;" under the preprocessor line so you no longer need to write "std::" each time you use it. If you opt for this method, the code would look like:

```
#include <iostream>

using namespace std;

int main()

{

        cout << "Hello World!";

        return 0;

}
```

Chapter 2 – C++ Variables and Operators

What You Will Learn:

**Introduction to C++ Operators and How to Use Them*

**Declaring and Determining the Value of Variables*

**Creating New Lines in the Program Output*

In a C++ program, variables and constants are controlled or "operated" using *Operators*. Take note that the basic operators in the C++ programming language are essentially the same as arithmetic operator. This includes the equal sign (=) for assigning expressions, the plus sign (+) for addition, the minus sign (-) for subtraction, the asterisk (*) for multiplication, the forward slash (/) for division, and the percentage sign (%) for obtaining the remainder from any expression.

C++ also uses other operators to fulfill additional tasks other than basic arithmetic operations. As mentioned in the previous chapter, the iostream header allowed you to use the insertion operator (<<) for processing output. There are also different operators accessible even without the #include directive. These "basic" operators can be categorized under *increment/decrement operators, comparison operators, compound assignment operators,* and *logical operators.*

Declaring Variables

Before using variables in C++ operations, you must first declare them and determine their values. Again, declaring variables and giving their values are two separate processes. The syntax for declaring variables are as follows:

"type" "variable";

Just like when initializing functions, you need to specify the data type to be used for a given variable. For example; say you want to declare "x" as an integer variable. The initialization should look like this:

int x;

After the declaration of x, you can give it a value using the assign operator (=). For example; to assign the value "99" to variable x, use the following line:

x = 99;

Make sure to declare a variable first before you assign a value to it. Alternatively, you can declare a variable and assign a value to it using a single line. This can be done using:

int x = 99;

Aside from setting these expressions as you write the program, you can also use operations and user input to determine their values as the program runs. But first, you need to learn about the other operators in C++.

Increment and Decrement Operators

The increment operator consists of two plus signs (++) while the decrement operator consists of two minus signs (--). The main purpose of increment and decrement operators is to shorten the expression of adding and subtracting 1 from any given variable. For example; if x = 2, then ++x should equal 3 while –x should equal 1.

If being used to determine the values of two or more variables, increment and decrement operators can be included as either a prefix or suffix. When used as a suffix (x++ or x--), it denotes the original value of x *before* adding or subtracting 1. When run on their own, both ++x and x++ have the same meaning. But when used in setting other variables, the difference is made obvious. Here is a simple example to illustrate the difference:

X = 5;

Y = ++x;

In this example, the value of y is determined *after* increasing the value of x. In other words, the value of y in this example is equal to 6.

X = 5;

Y = x++;

In this example, the value of y is determined *before* increasing the value of x. In other words, the value of y in this example is equal to 6.

Compound Assignment Operators

Aside from basic arithmetic operators and the standard assignment operator (=), compound assignment operators can also be used to perform an operation before a value is assigned. Compound assignment operators are basically shortened versions of normal expressions that use basic arithmetic operators.

Here are some examples of compound assignment operators:

x -= 1; // this is the same as the expression x = x − 1;

x *= y; // this is the same as the expression x = x * y;

x += 1;   // this is the same as the expression x = x + 1;

x /= y;   // this is the same as the expression x = x / y;

Comparison Operators

Variables and other expressions can be compared using relational or comparison operators. These operators are used to check whether a value is greater than, less than, or equal to another. Here are the comparison operators used in C++ and their description:

==   -   checks if the values are equal

<   -   checks if the first value is less than the second

>   -   checks if the first value is greater than the second

<=	-	checks if the first value is less than *or* equal to the second
>=	-	checks if the first value is greater than *or* equal to the second
!=	-	checks if the values are NOT equal

Comparison operators are commonly used in creating condition statements. They can also be used to evaluate an expression and return a *Boolean value* ("true" or "false"). Using the comparison operators listed above; here are some example expressions and their corresponding Boolean value:

(8 == 1) // this line evaluates to "false"

(8 > 1) // this line evaluates to "true"

(8 != 1) // this line evaluates to "true"

(8 <= 1) // this line evaluates to "false"

Also take note that the Boolean value "false" is equivalent to "0" while "true" is equivalent to other non-zero integers.

Aside from numerical values, the value of variables can also be checked when using comparison operators. Simply use a variable's identifier when creating the expression. Of course, the variable must be declared and given an identified value first before a valid comparison can be made. Here is an example scenario

```
#include <iostream>
using namespace std;

int main ()

{
        int a = 3;      // the values of a and b are set first
        int b = 4;
        cout << "Comparison a < b = " << (a < b);
        return 0;
}
```

The output for this code is as follows:

14

Comparison a < b = true

Take note that the insertion operator (<<) is used to insert the value of the expression "a < b" in the output statement, which is denoted in the 7th line ("cout << "Comparison a < b = "...). Don't forget that you *need an output statement* in order to see if your code works. The following code will produce no errors, but it won't produce an output either:

```
#include <iostream>

int main (

{
        int a = 3;
        int b = 4;
        (a < b);
        return 0;
}
```

In this code, it is also true that a < b. However, no output will be produced since the lines necessary for the program output are omitted.

Logical Operators

There are also other logical operators in C++ that can determine the values of Boolean data. They are the NOT (!), AND (&&), and OR (||) operators. Here are specific examples on how they are used:

!(6 > 2)   // the **NOT** operator (!) completely reverses any relational expressions and produces the opposite result. This expression is false because 6 > 2 is correct

(6 > 2 && 5 < 10) // the **AND** (&&) operator only produces true if both expressions correct. This expression is true because both 6 > 2 && 5 < 10 are correct

(6 = 2 || 5 < 10) // the **OR** (||) operator produces true if one of the expressions are correct. This expression is true because the 5 < 10 is correct although 6 = 2 is false.

You can also use the NOT operator in addition to the other two logical operators. For example:

!(6 = 2 || 5 < 10) // this expression is false

!(6 > 2 && 5 < 10) // this expression is also false

!(6 < 2 && 5 < 10) // this expression is true

Creating New Lines

From this point on in this book, you will be introduced to simple C++ programs that produce output with multiple lines. To create new lines when producing output, all you need to do is to use the *new line character* (\n). Alternatively, you can use the "endl;" manipulator to create new lines when using the "cout" code. The main difference is that the *internal buffer* for the output stream is "flushed" whenever you use the "endl;" manipulator with "cout". Here are examples on how to use both:

cout << "Sentence number one \nSentence number two";

The example above uses the new line character.

cout << "Sentence number one" << endl;
cout << "Sentence number two";

The example above uses "endl;".

Of course, the first code (using \n) is relatively simpler and easier for general output purposes. Both will produce the following output:

Sentence number one

Sentence number two

Chapter 3 – All About User Input

What You Will Learn:

**Utilizing the Input Stream

**Using Input to Determine or Modify Values

**How to Input and Output Strings

Up to this point, you've learned how to make a C++ program that can perform arithmetic operations, comparisons, and can produce output as well. This time, you will learn how to code one of the most important aspects of computer programs – *user input.*

As stated earlier, user input can be utilized to determine or modify the values of certain variables. C++ programs use abstractions known as *streams* to handle input and output. Since you already know about the syntax for output ("cout"), it's time to learn about the syntax for input ("cin").

The Extraction Operator

The input syntax "cin" is used with the *extraction operator* (>>) for formatted input. This combination along with the *keyboard* is the standard input for most program environments. Remember that you still need to declare a variable first before input can be made. Here is a simple example:

int x; // this line declares the variable identifier x. Take note of the data type "int" which means that only an integer value is accepted

cin >> x;   // this line extracts input from the cin syntax and stores it to x

User input can also be requested for multiple variables in a single line. For example; say you want to store integer values for variables x and y. This should look like:

int x, y;   // this line declares the two variables

cin >> x >> y;   // this line extracts user input for variables x and y

Take note that the program will automatically require the user to input *two* values for the two variables. Which comes first depends on the order of the variables in the line (in this case, input for variable "x" is requested first).

Here is an example of a program that extracts user input and produces an output:

#include <iostream>   // again, this is essential for input and output
using namespace std;

int main ()

{

    int x;
    cout << "Insert a random number \n";
    cin >> x;   // this is where user input is extracted
    cout << "You inserted: " << x;
    return 0;

}

Bear in mind that the value extracted from the input stream overwrites any initial value of a variable. For example, if the variable was declared as "int x = 2;" but was later followed by the statement "cin >> x;", the new value will then replace the original value until the program/function restarts or if an assignment statement is introduced.

Strings

Keep in mind that there are other types you can assign to variables in C++. Aside from integers, another fundamental type is the *string*. A string is basically a variable type that can store sets of characters in a specific sequence. In other words, this is how you can assign words or sentences as values for certain variables.

First of all, you need to add the preprocessor directive "#include <string>" before you can use strings in your program. Next, you need to declare a string before it can receive assignments. For example; if you want to declare a string for "Name" and assign a value for it, you can use the code:

```
#include <string>
using namespace std;

int main ()

{
    string name;
    name = "Insert your name here"; // including quotations

}
```

Creating output using strings is basically the same as with integers. You only need to use "cout" and insert the string to the line. The correct syntax is as follows:

string name;

Name = "Your Name Here";

cout << "My name is: " << name;

Without any changes, the output for the above code is:

Your Name Here

Inputting Strings

To allow user input values for strings, you need to use the function "getline" in addition to the standard input stream "cin". The syntax for this is "getline (cin, [string]);". Below is an example program that puts string input into application.

```cpp
#include <iostream>
#include <string>
using namespace std;

int main ()

{
        string name;
        cout << "Greetings! What is your name?\n";
        getline (cin, name); // this is the extraction syntax
        cout << "Welcome " << name;
        return 0;

}
```

Take note that strings have "blank" values by default. This means nothing will be printed if no value is assigned or if there is no user input.

Chapter 4 – Using Flow Control Statements

What You Will Learn:

**If and Else Selection Statements*

**Creating Choices*

**Creating Iterating/Looping Statements*

Remember that statements are the basic building blocks of a program written using C++. Each and every line that contains expressions such as a variable declaration, an operation, or an input extraction is a statement.

However, these statements are *linear* without some form of flow control that can establish the "sense" or "logic" behind a C++ program. This is why you should learn how to utilize flow control statements such as *selection statements* and *looping statements*.

If and Else Statements

If and else statements are the most basic form of logic in a C++ program. Basically, the main purpose of an "if" statement is to allow the execution of a specific line or "block" of multiple statements only *if* a specified condition is fulfilled.

Next is the "else" statement which allows you to specify what would occur in case the conditions aren't met. Without an "else" statement, everything inside the "if" statement will be completely ignored. Here the syntax for an "if" and "else" statement:

```
if (age >= 18)
        cout << "You are allowed to drink.";
```

else

    cout << "You are not yet allowed to drink.";

Remember that conditions can only be set using comparison operators and logical operators (refer to Chapter 2). Take note that you can also execute multiple statements using if/else conditions by enclosing the lines in curly braces. It is also possible to use composite conditions using logical operators such as AND (&&) and OR (||).

Finally, you can use another "if" statement after an "else" statement for even more possibilities. Of course, you also need to specify conditions for every "if" statement you use. Here is a good example that demonstrates what you can do using "if" and "else" statements in addition to user input:

```
#include <iostream>
using namespace std;

int main()

{
    int number;
    cout << "Enter a number from 1-3\n";
    cin >> number;
    if (number == 1 || number == 2)
        cout << "You have entered either 1 or 2.";
    else if (number == 3)
        cout << "You have entered 3.";
    else
    {
        cout << "Please follow the instructions\n";
        cout << "Please Try Again.";
    }
    return 0;
}
```

There are 3 possible outcomes in the program above. The first outcome is achieved if the user entered any of the numbers 1 or 2. The second outcome is achieved if the user entered the number 3. Lastly, the third outcome is achieved if the user entered a different number other the ones specified.

Creating Choices (Yes or No)

Another way to utilize if/else statements is to create "Yes or No" choices. For this, you need to make use of the variable type "char" which can hold a character from the *8-bit character set* (you can use char16_t, char32_t, or wchar_t for larger character sets; but this is not usually necessary). Just like all other variables, a "char" variable needs to be declared before it can be used.

Of course, you want the user to make the choice, which is why you need to use the "cin" function to extract user input. Here is a simple program that asks for the user's gender:

```
#include <iostream>
using namespace std;

int main()

{
        char gender; // this is the char variable declaration
        cout << "Male or Female? (M/F)";
        cin >> gender; // user input is stored to gender
        if (gender == 'm' || gender == 'M')
                cout << "You have selected Male.";
        else if (gender == 'f' || gender == 'F')
                cout << "You have selected Female.";
        else
                cout << "Please follow the instructions.";
        return 0;

}
```

Take note that you should use *single quotation marks* (') when pinpointing "char" values. In C++, "char" values are always called inside single quotation marks. Additionally, remember that "char" values are case-sensitive, which is why the example above used the OR (||) operator in the conditions to accept both lowercase and uppercase answers. You can see that the program above checked if the user entered 'm', 'M', 'f', or 'F'.

Looping Statements

Lastly, using "loops" allow statements to be executed for a set number of times or until a condition is met. By incorporating other statements in loops, you can do far more than just create pointless repetitions. But first, you need to be familiar with the different types of loops.

There are 3 types of loops in C++ -- *while, do,* and *for.*

While Loop

The *"while loop"* is regarded as the simplest form of loop in the C++. Basically, it repeats the statement(s) as long as the given condition is true. Keep in mind that your code should be structured to eventually fulfill the condition; otherwise you might create an "infinite loop".

Here is an example of a while loop:

```
int x = 100;

while (x >= 0)      // the condition for the loop is set
    {
    cout << x;
    --x;   // the value of x is decreased
    }
```

In this example, the loop executes as long as the value of x is greater than or equal to 0. Take note of the decrement operator (--) in the statement "--x;". This makes sure that the value of x is continually decreased until the condition is met and the loop ends.

Do-While Loop

The next type of loop is the *"do-while loop"*. The do-while loop is essentially the same as the while loop. The main difference is that the do-while loop allows the execution of the statement(s) at least *once* before the condition is checked. Whereas in the while loop, the condition is checked *first*.

Here is an example of a do-while loop:

```
int x = 100;
int y;

do
    {
    cout << "The value is " << x << "\n";
    cout << "Enter a value to subtract.";
    cin >> y;
    x -= y;
    }
while (x > 0);      // in the do-while loop, the condition is checked last
```

In the example above, the statements are executed at least once before the value of x is checked. Whereas in a while loop, there is a possibility that the statement(s) will not be executed at all.

For Loop

The third type of loop is the *"for loop"* which has specific areas for the *initialization, condition,* and *increase*. These three sections are sequentially executed throughout the life cycle of the loop. By structure, for loops are created to run a certain number of times because increment or decrement operators are usually used in the "increase" section.

Here is the syntax for this loop to help you understand it better:

for (int x = 10; x > 0; x--)

Notice the three expressions inside the parentheses (int x = 10; x > 0; x--) are separated in semicolons. These parameters denote the three sections of the loop. You may also use multiple expressions for each section using a comma (,). Here is the syntax for this:

```
for ( int x = 10, y = 0; x != y; --x, ++y )
    {
    cout << "X and Y is different\n";
    }
```

In this example, the loop is executed as long as x is not equal to y. And in order for the loop to end, the values of x and y are adjusted until the value of x equals the value of y. Based on the parameters above, the statement "X and Y is different" will run a total of 5 times before the loop is ended.

Conclusion

Thank you again for purchasing this book!

I hope this book was able to help you to learn and understand the C++ programming language!

The next step is to start from where you are now and try to learn something new. Keep in mind that you've only scratched the surface of all the things you can do in the world of C++!

Finally, if you enjoyed this book, please take the time to share your thoughts and post a review on Amazon. We do our best to reach out to readers and provide the best value we can. Your positive review will help us achieve that. It'd be greatly appreciated!

Thank you and good luck!

Book 2

Facebook Social Power
BY SAM KEY

The Most Powerful Represented Facebook Guide to Making Money on anything on the Planet!

Table Of Contents

Introduction

I want to thank you and congratulate you for purchasing the book, "Learning the Social Power of Facebook: The Most Powerful Represented Facebook Guide to Making Money on anything on the Planet!"

This book contains proven steps and strategies on how to learn ways to use Facebook as a means to generate money for whatever business you have.

As you well may know by now, Facebook can be an amazing tool to promote your business, and of course, make money from it. However, not everyone knows how to do it, but with the help of this book, you'll learn everything you need to know about how to use Facebook to attract people's attention, and be successful in the world of business.

What are you waiting for? Start reading this book now and make money through Facebook as soon as possible!

Thanks again for purchasing this book, I hope you enjoy it!

Chapter 1: Make Use of Advertising based on E-Commerce

Because of Facebook's Ad Platform, a lot of marketers have been able to reach a wide range of audience because they get to put ads on their Facebook Pages that takes those who click the links to E-Commerce sites, so just the fact that these people get to see their pages already add a lot of traffic to their sites, and may allow people to get paid.

Oftentimes, people overlook the ads-to-direct sites but knowing how to go forth with it is very beneficial because it has a three-way approach that will help you earn a lot of money. Basically, this approach goes as follows:

FB Ads—Discount Pages/Website Sales—Buyers/Customers

One example of a company that benefited a lot from E-Commerce based Advertising through Facebook is Vamplets.com. Vamplets.com is popular for selling plush dolls—but these dolls aren't just regular plush dolls, as they are Vampire Plushies. When Vamplets used this kind of advertising, they were able to achieve 300% ROI, which is definitely a mean feat.

So, how then are you going to be able to use E-Commerce based Advertising for your business? Follow the pointers below and you'll understand how.

Choose your Audience

First and foremost, you have to choose your target demographic so that sales funnel will be easier to be filled. Facebook will allow you to choose between one of the following:

- Custom Audience from Your Website

- Custom Audience from MailChimp

- Data File Custom Audience

- Custom Audience from Your Mobile App

Once you're able to choose your target demographic, it will be easy for you to convert an ad to money because these people will be interested in what you have to offer because you're no longer going to be generalizing things.

You can also choose your audience via the Facebook Audience Insights Category. Here, you'll be able to find people who are interested in your campaign, based on pages that they have liked, so that you'd know that they would like to see what your business is all about. This is called interest-based campaigning.

You can also try using Lookalike Audiences. You can do this by making use of your existing audience, and then pick the next group of people who act and feel similar to your original audience so your posts would be able to reach more people, and you'd get more traffic and revenue, as well. It would be nice to test audiences, too, so you'd know who's interested in your services.

For example, you're selling clothes for pregnant women. You really cannot expect people who are single or who are still in High School click your ads, or like your page, because of course, they're not in that stage of their lives yet. So, make sure that you choose audiences that you know will listen to what you have to say.

Then, go on and place a Facebook Pixel to the footer of your page, and your ads will then be connected to Facebook. You can also choose to send traffic to one audience group this week, then to another group the next.

Make Proper Segments for Visitors of Your Homepage

Of course, you have to make sure that your homepage gets the attention of many because if it doesn't, and if people feel alienated by it, you also cannot expect that you'll gain profit from it. The three basic things that you have to have in your homepage include:

- New Sales Items

- Branding Ads

- Other Promotional Ads

Make Segments for Categories and Products

You can also place ads in various categories of your website so that even if your customer does not check out all the items he placed in the cart, your website will still gain some revenue because more often than not, customers like to buy products based on ads that were able to get through to them.

Chapter 2: Use Fan Marketing E-Commerce

Basically, Fan Marketing E-Commerce is the means of promoting your business by making sure that you post ads through your page and have those ads appear on the newsfeeds of your target demographic.

Research has it that fans become more interested in a new product or business when they see ads, instead of when they learn about the said products through contests or just from other people. Why? Simply because ads are more professional ways of getting people's attention and marketing products, and Facebook definitely makes that easy.

However, it's not enough that you just have a fanpage. You have to make sure that you actually use the said page and that it doesn't get stuck. You can do this by making sure that you constantly post a thing or two, and that you interact with your fans, as well.

You see, a study held in 2011 showed that although over a hundred thousand people may like a certain page, sometimes, revenue only gets up by 7%, because the owners of the fan pages do not interact with their fans and have not posted anything in a while. You also have to make sure that you stay relevant by being able to attract new fans from time to time.

Once you do this right, you'll be able to create the process of:

FB Ads—FB Fans—See Posts—Click to Website—Buyers/Customers

Some of those who have greatly benefited from Fan Marketing Strategies include:

- Baseball Roses, a company that sells artificial roses made from old baseball balls, who gained over 437% of ROI with the help of Facebook Fan Marketing;

- Superherostuff.com, a website that sells merchandise based on famous superheroes, such as t-shirts, jackets, hoodies, shoes, and more, gained over 150% ROI, and;

- Rosehall Kennel Breeds, a company that specializes in selling German Shepherds, gained over a whopping 4,000% of ROI for its fan acquisition speed alone—and that's definitely something that should inspire you.

So, what exactly did these companies do and how did they make use of Facebook Fan Marketing E-Commerce for their own benefit? Here are some tips that you can follow:

1. **Make sure that you post a new update after your last update is gone from people's newsfeeds.** Sometimes, you see posts in your feed for even a day or two after posting, but there are also times when they are

gone after just a couple of minutes or hours. It actually varies due to how fans see or react on those posts and Facebook's EdgeRank Algorithm will be able to give you a glimpse of how your post is doing, based on three main factors, which are:

 a. **Likes per Post.** You'd know that people are interested in your posts when they actually make it a point to like the said posts, and it's great because likes are always updated in real time, and will also let your posts stay longer on people's newsfeeds. Therefore, make sure to check the numbers of likes regularly.

 b. **Comments per Post.** Comments are always time-stamped, but you cannot always rely on these as not everyone like to comment on posts, and you cannot define whether the posts appear on people's feeds, or they're simply too lazy to comment.

 c. **Impressions per Post.** This is basically the number of times a single status has been viewed. While the numbers update as more and more people get to see your post, there are also times when the number stay stagnant only because Facebook refuses to update, so may have to wait a while to see the real numbers.

A good way of trying to gauge your influence on Facebook is by posting an hourly status, then make sure that you record the number of likes, comments, and impressions, and then record the data on Excel. Make a graph, then see the ratio of how much your posts appear on one's feeds, and decide the average number of posts that you have to do per day or per week.

2. **Make sure that the things you post are not redundant.** People these days have really short attention span so it would be nice if you know how to post varied content. Make sure that your fans have something to come back to each day, and that they don't get bored with whatever it is that you have on your website and won't click the "dislike" button.

3. **Do some marketing.** Again, you're trying to make money by means of promoting your products so you have to do a lot of marketing via Facebook. An easy way of doing this is by giving your fans discount codes that they can use if they're interested in buying your products so that they'd constantly check your page.

4. **Make sure that social sharing buttons are open.** While you may use Facebook as the original platform for advertising your services, you also have to realize that it's important to share your content on other websites or social networking sites so that more people would get to see what you have to offer. Also, make sure that your page is set to public because you really cannot expect people to know what you want them to know if your page is set to private. When your page is public, they'll be able to like, comment, and share your posts, which will bring you more traffic and

more revenue. Then, connect your Facebook Page to your other social media accounts so that whenever you post updates on your Facebook Page, the updates will be sent to all your other accounts, as well.

5. **Don't ever try hard-selling tactics.** It's always better to be subtle because people hate it when they feel like their feeds are full of pages that just sell their products outright without making the fans understand what they're all about. So, try asking your fans some questions, or create polls about what kind of products or services they like but never just put up ads or ask them to "buy your products" right away without helping them know that you're their "friend" and that you want them to know what's best in the market right now. You can also place behind the scenes videos of what goes on in your company, or post testimonials from past customers to get the curiosity of your fans running. This way, you get to be trustworthy and your business will be more authoritative, and people would be more interested.

6. **And, make sure that you provide good customer service.** For a Facebook Page to be successful, it doesn't have to be bombarded with ads, you also have to make sure that you get to be friends with your customers and that loyalty and trust are built. For example, when one of your fans posts questions or queries on your page, take time to answer the said questions, and make sure that you reply as soon as possible so that you get to create some sense of urgency and that people will know that you're there.

Keep these tips in mind and you'll surely be able to make use of your Facebook Page to give you a lot of profit. Oh, and make sure to have ample amounts of patience, too!

Chapter 3: Connect Facebook Ads to E-Mail

Another way of making use of Facebook to gain revenue is by connecting ads to e-mails. Basically, it's a way of promoting content to your e-mail subscribers so that it will be easier for your fans to know about your new products or services, or to know if there are contests or events coming up based on the updates that you have sent.

Basically, when Facebook ads are sent to people's e-mails, there are more chances of acquiring a larger number of future subscribers. And Facebook makes this easy for you as they have a feature that allows you to add E-mail lists to your Fan Page so that whenever you post an update, your e-mail list will automatically get to know it, too.

The target formula is as follows:

FB Ad—Squeeze—E-mail Sign Up—E-mail Open—E-mail Click to Visit—Buyers/Customers

So, in order for you to be successful in this kind of marketing tactic, you first have to get a target demographic of e-mail subscribers. While it may be easy to just post an invite so your fans would want to be part of your e-mail list, it will be nice to filter people who probably won't open your e-mails and choose people who would be interested in what you have to offer. You can do this by adding information to the Facebook Ad Copy Page. The information that you need are as follows:

- Gender

- Age

- Location

- Interests

- Relationship Status

- Educational Attainment/Level

- Workplace

- Pages that have been liked (So you'd get to see if they would like the posts that you'd be making)

Then, go on and upload the e-mail list on your Facebook Page by giving Facebook a list of e-mails from MailChimp or any other AutoResponder Service, so that the e-mail addresses of your fans will be synchronized to your page.

Effective Message Integration

It's so easy to send a message but it's never really easy to make sure that those messages are effective. However, there are a couple of tips that you can keep in mind:

- Optimize Facebook Ad Headlines with Catchy Subject Lines so that your fans will be interested to open your e-mails. Examples include:

    o Do Gamers dream of DOTA II?

    o Why your 12 year old likes Miley Cyrus

    o 8 Most Annoying Social Media Moments of 2014

    o 3 Ways to Improve Your Life

    Basically, you have to make sure that your subject lines have a lot to do with your content and with your line of business so that your fans won't be confused and they'd be interested in what you have to say.

- Add your fans' testimonials and comments about your services so others would know that you are for real.

- Add images into your e-mails. After all, people have short attention span and they would appreciate it if they get to see images as part of your e-mails because these would get their attention more and would help them picture what you are talking about.

- Let your fans know that you are going to send another e-mail blast by updating your Facebook status.

- Tease some of the contents of your e-mail on your status updates so that your fans will be hyped up and will be curious to open their e-mails.

- Make use of Facebook Landing Tabs, and Social Log-in Software, so that whenever your fans open their e-mails, it will automatically add traffic to your Facebook Page, and your website, as well.

- Put some sort of disclaimer, or a line that allows your fans to unsubscribe if they want to, because they have to know that you're not actually forcing them to read your messages and that they have the choice to unsubscribe from your list.

- And don't forget to send Thank You messages. If you want to foster a great relationship with your fans, you have to let them know that you're thankful that they're around, and that they're part of your list, so that they will realize that it's substantial to read the content that you are sending, and that it's important to be a fan of yours, instead of just talking about yourself all the time, without thinking of your fans. After all, without them, you won't gain any profit so you have to be grateful that they're around.

You can also run Geo-targeted ads, or ads that are meant for people who live in one location alone, so that the e-mails would feel more personal and so that your fans will know that you are really thinking of them. Sometimes, targeting people who are in the same vicinity as you is more effective because you get to really connect with them as you experience the same things and you'd know that they are more likely to try your products, unlike those that live in far away places.

If you're able to be successful with Facebook E-mail marketing, you can definitely gain more traffic and more revenue. One of those Fortune 500 Companies actually gained 400% ROI just because of its e-mail subscribers, so you can expect that you'll gain more, too, but only if you follow the tips given above. Good Luck!

Chapter 4: Making Use of Your Ad-Supported Sites

Ad-Supported sites are those that run advertisements and allow the said ads to be shared to your Facebook Page.

This is especially helpful for those whose businesses are really situated online, and those whose blogs or websites are their bread and butter. So, if that's the case, it would be important to create a Facebook Page that's connected to your blog or your website so that things would be formalized more. People like it when they see that a certain website has a Facebook Page because they feel like they'd get to be updated more without having to go to the website.

The formula for this is as follows:

FB Ad—FB Fan—See Post—Click to Website—Click Ad

So basically, when people click ads on your website that take them to your Facebook Page and Vice Versa, you not only gain traffic, you get to be paid, as well. This is similar as the popular Pay-Per-Click Advertising tactic. And also, when you get more fans from various parts of the world, your revenue will increase even more mainly because your content now gets to reach a large number of people, which evidently is beneficial for your business.

Proud Single Moms, a site targeted to help single mothers, gained over $5,000 for Facebook Ads alone that were promoted on their Facebook Page that has around 100,000 fans. On their blog, they made sure that they posted topics that single mothers would be able to relate to, and they also made sure that they used keywords that would give them high search rank on search engines such as Google, or Yahoo.

You can make use of Keyword Tools that are found online to find the perfect keywords that are related to your niche. Once you use these keywords in your posts, you'll be able to generate traffic and revenue.

The main reason why ads on Facebook are so effective is the fact that almost everyone in the world has a Facebook account, so of course, you can expect them to see your posts and the ads that are on your page, too. Plus, when you post links of your blog's content to your Facebook Page, there are more chances that people will get to read these posts because of course, they found it on Facebook, and they didn't use the web just so they could see your website. And these days, that is very important. The key is to be reachable.

Proud Single Moms made sure that they posted the links of blog post updates each day and in just a matter of six months, they were able to create another website that gave them more revenue.

Chapter 5: Other Tips

Aside from the techniques given above, you can also make use of these Facebook Marketing tactics to make sure that your business gains more profit:

Ads through SMS

While it may not be as popular as other Facebook Marketing tips, the combination of Facebook Ads and Text Messaging have slowly been gaining the attention of many for being a fast-paced approach when it comes to advertising products and services. In fact, around 24% of marketers on mobile have gained more ROI just because people have responded to text messages regarding product promotions, and have tried the coupons that they gave away through text, too.

This is especially effective for those with business that are related to food as free coupons that were sent to Facebook fans helped these fans to be more interested to try certain products that were being sold, and have visited the restaurants more often in hopes that they'd be given more information and more freebies, too. When people feel like they know the latest news about a certain establishment or a certain product, it's easy for them to appreciate the said establishment and so they get to patronize it more. This then gave the restaurants around $60,000 more revenue, which is definitely something good!

Give Some Offers that they won't be able to refuse!

Mostly everyone want freebies, because money is really hard to come by these days and not everything is affordable, so of course, they feel like it's nice to be able to get some goodies or services for free. Facebook Offers actually help you create deals with your fans that are not available on other social media platforms.

Basically, you ask your customers to like your page and leave their e-mail addresses so that you can send them coupons or offers that they can redeem in your store. First, make the offers exclusive to your fans then when it gets successful, you can then make more offers for people outside your circle so that more people would be excited to try your products and see what you have to offer.

Don't think about losing profit. More often than not, when you give things away for free, people will be more interested to try your other products and so of course, they'd be paying you in the future, so it's like you have made them your investment and soon enough, you'll benefit from them.

Create Apps for them

A lot of people these days rely on apps that they could use to open certain websites or pages, and of course, if you create an app for your business, it will be easy for them to read your content and it will be easy for you to reach them. They wouldn't have to deal with the hassle of using the browser just so they could see some offers or read articles connected to a certain topic that they would like to learn about. Also, it's better if you add links to your Facebook Page to the app that you have created so that everything will be merged together.

You can also create Facebook Ads without creating a Facebook Page

You can do this by selecting the Clicks to Website option of Facebook or the Website Conversions tab. People will still get to see your ads on the right side of their pages. You know, those ads that appear near the chat sidebar, so in a way, you still get to promote your business, but having Facebook Pages are still way better because then the ads appear on the main feeds and not just on the right side tabs.

Create a catchy headline

Just like how important it is to create effective e-mail subject lines, it's also important to create catchy ad headlines because these will attract people's attention and will allow people to understand what you and your business are all about.

The rule of thumb is to make sure that the headline of your ad is the same as the title of your page so it will be easily recognizable. It would also be helpful if you pair it up with an image that you have created so that people will be able to connect the said image to your business and it will be easy for them to remember your ad.

Make use of Sponsored Stories, too

You see, sponsored stories are the results of how people interact on your page or how they appreciate your content. Basically, whenever someone likes your posts or updates, or when they comment on or share your content, it creates "Facebook Stories". To make sure that these stories appear on a lot of people's newsfeeds, you have to pay a minimal fee, so it's like you get to easily advertise your content and you make sure that people actually get to see them.

But make sure that you choose the best bidding and advertising options

What's good about Facebook is that it allows you to choose the best kind of bidding option that will be good for your business. For example, you can choose whether you want to gain revenue through clicks, or through impressions then you can then reach your objective after you have customized your bids.

You can also choose whether you'd like to pay for your content to be advertised by paying daily, or by paying for a lifetime. The advantages of paying for a lifetime is that you'd know that your content will always be published and that you'd basically have nothing else to worry about, but the thing is that when you want to change the products you are advertising or if you're going to close your business down, it's like you'll get people confused because they'll still see ads from your old site, and they'd keep looking for your services. So, it's recommended that you just pay for the ads daily or on a case to case basis, say there's an event that's coming up and the like, so that it won't be hard for you to reach your followers and gain potential fans in the process, too.

When making use of image ads, make sure that text is only 20%

You would not want to bombard your followers with too many texts and images in just one post. Plus, your image ads won't be approved if they contain more than 20% of text.

In order to know if your ads are following Facebook's guidelines, check out the Facebook Grid Tool that will help you see how your ad looks and what needs to be changed, if necessary.

Let others help you

Sometimes, two heads are better than one, and it's great because when you add another admin to your page, they can also update your page so whenever you're busy or if you cannot answer queries right away, these other admins can help you out.

Just make sure that you choose admins that you can trust and that they know a lot about your business so the things they will be posting will be substantial, too. To do this, just go to the Ad Manager option of Facebook, then click Ad Account Roles, and choose Add a User. Make sure that the person you will add as an admin is your friend on Facebook and that his e-mail address can easily be searched through Facebook, too.

And, don't forget to choose the revenue model that is right for you

To do this, you may have to try each technique first, but don't worry because sooner or later, you'll find the one that proves to be the most effective for your business.

In the marketing business, trial and error really is one of the biggest keys to success, so don't worry if you feel like you aren't being successful right away. Take chances and soon enough, you'll be on the path to success. Good Luck!

Conclusion

Thank you again for purchasing this book!

I hope this book was able to help you understand how you can use Facebook to advertise your business and gain lots of revenue.

The next step is to follow the techniques listed here, and don't be afraid to try each one because sooner or later, you'll find the perfect fit for you. Advertise through Facebook and let your business soar!

Thank you and good luck!

Check Out My Other Books

Below you'll find some of my other popular books that are popular on Amazon and Kindle as well. Simply click on the links below to check them out. Alternatively, you can visit my author page on Amazon to see other work done by me.

Android Programming in a Day

Python Programming in a Day

C Programming Success in a Day

C Programming Professional Made Easy

JavaScript Programming Made Easy

PHP Programming Professional Made Easy

C ++ Programming Success in a Day

Windows 8 Tips for Beginners

HTML Professional Programming Made Easy

If the links do not work, for whatever reason, you can simply search for these titles on the Amazon website to find them.

www.ingramcontent.com/pod-product-compliance
Lightning Source LLC
Chambersburg PA
CBHW060930050326
40689CB00013B/3037